Table of

.... 1

Table of Contents 5

Introduction 6

Chapter 1: Techniques to Understand Your Teenage Son 13

Chapter 2: Fostering Creativity 23

Chapter 3: Handling Anger as a Parent 39

Chapter 4: Methods to Discipline Teen Boys 44

Chapter 5: Creating A Good Environment to Raise Teens ... 50

Chapter 6: A Parent's Survival Guide to Teenage Boys 65

Conclusion 93

Other Books You'll Love! 97

REFERENCES 101

Parenting Teen Boys

in Today's Challenging World

Proven Methods for Improving Teenagers Behaviour with Whole Brain Training

Bukky Ekine-Ogunlana

© **Copyright Bukky Ekine-Ogunlana 2021 – All rights reserved.**

The content contained within this book may not be reproduced, duplicated or transmitted without direct written permission from the author or the publisher.

Under no circumstance will any blame or legal responsibility be held against the publisher, or author, for any damages, reparation, or monetary loss due to the information contained within this book. Either directly or indirectly. You are responsible for your own choices, actions and results.

Legal Notice:

This book is copyright protected. This book is only for personal use. You cannot amend, distribute, sell, use, quote or paraphrase any part, or the content within this book, without the author or publisher's consent.

Disclaimer Notice:

Please note the information contained within this document is for educational and entertainment purpose only. All effort has been executed to present accurate, up to date, and reliable, complete information. No warranties of any kind are declared or implied. Readers acknowledge that the author is not engaging in the rendering of legal, financial, medical or professional advice. The content within this book has been derived from various sources. Please consult a licensed professional before attempting any techniques outlined in this book

By reading this document, the reader agrees that under no circumstances is the author responsible for any losses, direct or indirect, which are incurred as a result of the use of the information contained within this document, including, but not limited to, —errors, omissions, or inaccuracies.

DEDICATION

This book is dedicated to our three amazing children and all the beautiful children worldwide who have passed through the T.C.E.C 6-16 years programme over the years. Thank you for the opportunity to serve you and invest in your colourful and bright future.

Introduction

Parenting has undeniably evolved over the years. With social media and the rise of technology, these aspects have significantly impacted how we raise our children. We are exposed to new, creative, and unique ways to parent our children. These have had incredible benefits for parents worldwide as we navigate the challenges presented through parenting with a community of other parents for support and encouragement. However, on the downside, it offers some avenues for you to take as a parent to raise your child that can be overwhelming, confusing, and doubly daunting.

While there is no "one size fits all" approach to parenting, nor is there a single formula that will apply to every child, there are cardinal rules that are encouraged, especially throughout this book and its companion book explicitly geared towards raising teen girls. Along every stage within your child's life, one of the main cardinal rules is for you, the parent, to evolve alongside your children. You simply would not apply the same parenting techniques on a toddler onto your teenager, as much your teenager may sometimes test your patience as a toddler would. While your children mature and face new social situations and experience the myriad of new emotions that life presents them, they, in turn, experience personal growth of their own that parents have to grapple with quickly to develop their parenting techniques alongside them. This often poses a challenge for parents around the world because as much as parenting means adopting the role of a guide to steer your child through the various challenges that life presents, it also means going through a form of growth yourself, a notion that is quite often neglected when it comes to discussing parenting.

As an adult, growth is often overlooked because adults are seen as seemingly all-knowing and planned for the world ahead of them. Ultimately, growth and evolution are sure ways to develop as an adult and show your children that life is a never-ending series of tests of your strength and courage. Parents often fall into the trap of posing as an authoritative dictator-type figure in their child's life by being overly strict or adopting a "helicopter parent" style. Or the opposite can occur, where parents are simply too laid-back and hands-off when it comes to raising their children. Sometimes this can unintentional, or a consequence of parents attempting to navigate through the endless decisions they have to make for their kids. Many parents start this way, but the most crucial part is that they choose to evolve. They acknowledge the mistakes they are making and decide to grow and learn from them. This is the biggest lesson to take out of this book. You may apply the techniques and strategies presented in this book closely and strictly yet find that your child is not responding accordingly. The next step is to try another method and continue adapting and learning from this process. This is the single most generous tip that we can impart to parents: parenting is a process and takes time and growth.

Making mistakes while parenting will always happen as you attempt to raise your children to become good citizens. This is inevitable, and many parents grapple with this, even if their children are older and have been parenting for years. The fear of mistakes often holds parents back, which in turn can hinder your child's development. It is a complicated and scary feat for adults who have children, bearing this responsibility is no small task. Most parents are determined to raise their children to the best of their ability and present them with opportunities to grow and develop from fledgelings into fully-grown adults. With that intent, they are faced with the question of *how* exactly to go about this. This book is a response to this very question.

Seasoned parents would argue that teenagerhood is the most challenging time for parenting. Many parents might say that this period for your teenagers is a time of high emotions and added pressure as your teenager experience leaving their childhood and are on the cusp of adulthood. Your teens are in the process of making big decisions that will affect their futures, particularly with their educations and careers, which is an incredibly stressful time for most. Teens could be experiencing more complex relationships and the emotions associated with that. Additionally, as your children age, they become more accustomed to the fact that the world is more flawed than what they might have been used to during their protected childhood years that featured a far more idealistic and optimistic view. As your children age, they are met with the responsibilities they will have to take on as adults. With all of these in mind, the immense stress that can weigh on a teen's mental health during this time can be immense. With this age transition being so formative and crucial for your teens, the same stress and pressure reflect on parents, which is why teenagerhood is a tough time for both parents and children alike.

Yet these years also bring some new joys. As your children are now ageing, they are grasping a better understanding of adulthood which means that they can more accurately empathize with their parents and build a new facet to the parent and child dynamic as they form their own opinions and experience the world differently but can articulate and share their thoughts with you. This aspect is a joy for many parents, as they can develop a friendship and more profound respect for their children as they view them in the different light that maturity brings. Parents often find that they can share more with their children at this age, which is crucial for fostering a healthy relationship. Like most things, teenagerhood has its own set of positives and qualms for both parents and teens alike.

The most crucial point that will consistently be reiterated is that no two children are the same. Every child experiences their surrounding environment differently and has their notions of the world they are raised in. Likewise, all children perceive themselves differently, and parents must respect this. These books are framed through gender, with the first part catered to raising teen girls, while the second part is geared towards raising teen boys. Understand that gender stereotypes can be extremely harmful to children. There is no right way to "act like a boy" or "act like a girl". These are incredibly dangerous ideas that parents must avoid when raising their Children because it fosters limitations on your children simply because of their gender. While there are rules that exist in society, what also exist simultaneously is fluidity. The concept of gender is a slippery slope. Still, it is ultimately up to parents to lay a firm groundwork and foundation to build confidence within their children to accept themselves despite societal expectations. It is up to dads and moms to teach their children that what they may like or dislike is simply due to their preferences and not a weakness. For example, if your son dislikes sports, it does not make him any less of a boy, let alone a man.

The parts of this book are divided by gender to play on the multi-dimensionality that is gender roles. Gender roles are an incredibly complex and intricate social conceptualization as it deems a range of attributed and desirable behaviours based on a person's sex. This way of thinking can be dangerous and certainly place limitations on your children. As much as we discourage gender stereotyping, there are a few inherent differences between boys and girls that should be differentiated and discussed when raising girls and boys. However, keep in mind that all of the tips are interchangeable between genders and can be applied to any child as they have no prerequisites or preconditions that need to be followed before being used. These tips are universally applicable and serve to nurture your teen's interests and needs, regardless of gender.

After reading this guide, please feel free to leave a review based on your findings and how useful the guide was to you. I would be incredibly thankful if you could take 60 seconds to write a brief review on the platform of purchase, even if it's just a few sentences!

12

Chapter 1: Techniques to Understand Your Teenage Son

W hen raising teen boys and teen girls, some fundamental differences exist. Some of these differences begin within the household, where boys are given less affection than their girl counterparts or allowing aggression and violent play by relying on the mantra of "boys will be boys". This is a slippery slope, as these notions that are seemingly innocent at the time can fester and develop into full psychological roadblocks that your children will have to face in their adulthood. These differences between genders are further fostered when your child enters the education system, mainly through the many education systems that segregate boys and girls during physical education classes. While education systems differ worldwide, the school system is often where these notions of gender and the applicable stereotypes are established with your child. By the time your child has entered their teen years, ideas of "running like a girl" or "acting like a boy" have firmly wormed their way into their mindset. It is an inevitable result of the education system.

What becomes vital here is how parents pick up on what their child is learning and either nip these ideas in the bud or turn them into learning lessons to show them a different world scope. By doing so, you are setting your teenager up to be prepared for a world of diversity. You are also teaching them essential life lessons by imparting that they are simply not limited to the conditions of their gender.

Here are some techniques to employ to gather an understanding of how your teen boy may perceive themselves. This is the first step to deciphering how you might want to raise your teen boy and the techniques you wish to employ to foster their interests.

1. Have a Good Relationship

Having a relationship with your children is incredibly important, and this is a known fact for every parent. A prerequisite to even begin to help your children deal with the number of things they are facing through their teenage years is to have a strong foundation and shared respect. With the teen years being so divisive and stress-filled, meeting these challenges with parents by their side is incredibly crucial for teens. Similarly, knowing when your children are going through hard times or maybe at crossroads begins with a strong relationship that allows open communication and provides a safe space.

2. Be Observant

Being proactive in your child's education and being aware of what they are being taught in their education is extremely important. For many parents, this may be a no-brainer, while some parents naively leave their children's education completely in the hands of their teachers. While teachers are incredibly vital and provide an insurmountable amount of support during your children's most formative years, playing a role in your Child's education is equally just as important. Growing a relationship with your child's teacher and keeping tabs on where they are thriving academically can help considerably tailor your parenting techniques towards them. Additionally, teachers are an excellent source for understanding how your teen may be doing socially and mentally, which will provide the next steps that may need to be taken to provide the support and help they need.

3. Show Affection

Particularly in the boys' case, many parents make the mistake of feeding their daughters more affection than their sons to foster a sense of masculinity from a young age. This idea of affection and masculinity being tied is hugely problematic and can lead to plenty of issues down the line. Masculinity and tenderness are not tied together, and boys deserve as much love and affection that girls receive in their lifetime. Demonstrating warmth and affection to all your children equally, regardless of gender, allows them to do the same for their children and avoid some of the issues that can arise from not experiencing love from parental figures.

1. Avoid the "boys will be boys" mentality

This dangerous mentality is often used as an excuse to brush off certain behaviours or attitudes seen in boys. This is definitely a slippery slope as it can foster violent tendencies and aggression that parents encourage as male behaviour. It allows unconscious biases to form and will enable boys to have a different framework of acceptable behaviours and attitudes that differs from girls. In other words, it gives them an excuse to engage in what could perhaps be inappropriate or unacceptable behaviour in the future. Using this phrase simply brushes off these impulses and is often used in specific bullying cases, which can be extremely harmful. It does not teach children that their actions are wrong and completely unacceptable. Instead, it gives them an excuse and a way out of facing real consequences and learning from their mistakes.

5. Be present

As much as your teenage son is growing up and becoming more and more mature every single day, while parents are expected to loosen the reins, it by no means entails completely abandoning parenting altogether. You represent a guide for your child to follow and model after, even into their adult lives. Being present in their lives means continuing the relationship and bond you share, even if you may feel like they simply do not need you anymore. This is hardly ever the case when parents are evolving and growing alongside their children. Parents can simultaneously allow their children to flourish on their terms while having a constant presence in their lives. This comes down to finding a balance and respecting the boundaries that your child imposes. While you may not like it at first, part of the process of being a parent is accepting hard to swallow pills like this and understanding that there will come a time where you will feel unwanted, but that certainly is not the case or the intention. What this means is your children are growing up and becoming adults themselves.

6. Nurture self-expression

Limiting your sons only to express themselves within a masculinity framework greatly hinders their development and can put your relationship with them in risk. Rather than encouraging rigid binaries of masculinity and femininity, allow your children to gravitate towards their likes and dislikes. These can manifest in some ways, from hobbies to the relationships they have. The critical aspect of this is to always keep in mind to nurture these habits by showing your support and respect towards your child's ways of self-expression, regardless of how it may manifest while you watch to know how to help. Every child grows and develops differently, so expecting your child to be just like your neighbour's son not only places unnecessary pressure on your son but also sets you up for failure and disappointment. Rather than encouraging your child to emulate other people, allow your son to come into their own and become their person. It mostly lies in parents to foster this sense of self-confidence and respect for themselves. As your child ages, they will be more accustomed and open with who they are, and thus more willing to share with you what they are experiencing mentally, emotionally, and socially as their parents.

7. Foster emotionality

Boys are often encouraged not to show their emotions, so the stereotype is that girls are more emotional than boys. While this is a vast generalization, there is some truth to it, and we may consider why this is the case. The basis for this lies in the fact that boys are simply told to put on a façade of rigidity and strength, where crying is now seen as a weakness. This, aside from being completely false, is dangerous as it encourages boys to bottle up their emotions which can lead to them spilling out in the most dangerous of situations. Rather than encourage your children to put on a brave face all the time, allow your boys to cry and experience the relief of dispelling their emotions in this way. Crying can be a healthier coping mechanism that can prevent your teens from turning to drugs or alcohol as a coping mechanism. The important part is to talk to your children after the fact and try to work out the extreme emotions they may be feeling. This has the most significant impact on your teens as they develop an understanding that their parents will always be a constant beacon of support.

8. Be a guide

Your children look to you as their role models from the minute they are brought into this world. This is simply what parenting is. But as they age, and especially by their teen years, inevitably your children will have more influences and face other figures who will significantly impact their lives. Respect this aspect, but also never relinquish your role as a guide to your children because ultimately you are still their parents. Always model behaviours that you are proud of and respect because your children will model the same after you, whether consciously or not. Knowing that you have set your standards for behaviours and attitudes in your household is a great way to find anomalies and notice how your child may be negatively influenced.

9. Family

The family dynamic can significantly benefit your children because every person plays an important role in raising a teen. We have all overheard of the African proverb "It takes a village to raise a child", and this rings true when it comes to helping your children thrive and be the best that they can be. Parents and siblings of an Individual play their roles by positively impacting an individual's life, so when it comes to understanding what your teen may be going through, relying on the different dynamics that may exist in your household is a way to ease some of the pressure a single parent may be experiencing. Siblings can tap into a different side of your struggling kid in a way that parents might not be able to. As much as the responsibility mainly lies on parents to bear the brunt of the weight of helping their children, there is also nothing wrong with relying on grandparents, the people around you to help out and play their role too.

10. Express how you feel

As your teens are older and more mature, they can relate to the emotions you may be feeling more so than they would have as a child. Being open and vulnerable to your children is an essential factor in getting them to open up themselves. Rather than bottling your own emotions up, show your children that everyone faces extreme experiences as well and this will allow them to see that everyone also goes through things and will therefore not feel as alone. While this is a way to show your children the realities that adults face, it does not mean putting added pressure and burdening them with the problems you are faced with. This is another means for your child to relate to you and therefore feel encouraged to share their own life more openly and willingly with you.

11. Professional help

Consider speaking to a professional if you find that you cannot grasp what your teen might be going through, whether it is because of reluctance on your teen's part to share or if the issue is more serious than you can help him manage. There is no shame in seeking professional help because it gives your teen a neutral party to speak to who provides a safe, judgment-free space for them to express themselves. This does not mean you are any less of a parent; it makes you a commendable one for recognizing your strengths and weaknesses and ultimately placing your child's health over your ego. Many parents struggle with the blow that their ego faces for they believe that speaking to a professional means that they are not a good parent. This is not the case. Many teens recognize their parents' limitations and appreciate the degree of seriousness they treat their mental health.

The severity of what your child may be going through can vary in degrees. Ultimately, it is up to you to take the right steps and help them express their feelings and manage their emotions appropriately in a sustainable and relieving way. Mental health is crucial for a teen during this age, so take it incredibly seriously and be proactive in helping your teen.

Chapter 2: Fostering Creativity

P lacing limitations on your teen boys on what they can or cannot do can be incredibly discouraging. Helping them find their passions can be one of the more exciting parts of parenting. As you expose your child to the possibilities of the world, they are learning a great deal about themselves and finding themselves. Hobbies are one of the most acceptable ways to do this. Traditionally, parents would limit their children in sports because of the idea of masculinity.

Nonetheless, as we have progressed as a society and continue to disregard these gendered ideas, it opens teen boys up to an endless world of new things to develop the creative and logical sides that can stay with them well into adulthood and for the rest of their lives. Fostering creativity for teen boys can often stump parents because they are still thinking in the framework of gender, where certain activities are exclusive to girls only. But when we rid of this idea altogether, we can see that there are plenty of options to foster creativity.

Some parents might question the need to foster creativity. Ultimately, it lies in the fact that we have some inclination towards creativity, expression, and the arts as humans. There are plenty of benefits to encourage your children to be creative, and there are plenty. With TV and computer screens more commonly becoming the object of your kids' obsession during their teen years, fostering creativity is a great way to primarily, get them away from their reliance on video games and watching TV all day. Creative development is a great way to teach your children how to think outside of the box and solve problems. Teens can develop their reasoning and logic as well as formulate their ideas independently without interference from teachers or their parents. Creativity opens up a whole world of possibilities for your children to explore art, dance, music, and many more. As children age, what can sometimes happen is that creativity is placed on the back burner as they face more intense curriculums in school. However, the need for creativity will most certainly come up during their adult life. Fostering divergent thinking from a young age will help them when they enter the workplace or higher education as they will be met with a multitude of challenges and hardships that will require thinking outside of the box. This is why parents must continue encouraging creative thinking and recognize the value of the benefits that arise out of this early on in parenting journey and your child's development.

One parent shared how helping her son develop creatively opened up many new traits and characteristics in her son that she never knew he was capable of. This newfound confidence was a breath of fresh air that changed the course of her son's life because he was no longer anti-social and afraid of socializing. Many activities are listed below that you can consider enrolling your children into. For this parent's son named Jake, he was interested in theatre but never found the confidence to take it seriously and pursue it. The parent, named Mary, found herself at wits' end because she could not seem to get her son to engage with her, no matter what she tried. She eventually found that she had to relinquish her hold on her son and allow him to flourish creatively by himself. This experience was resisted at first. Jake was so set in his ways that he did not want to partake in new activities or meet new people. But Mary had given him an ultimatum because he was spending all of his time locked up in his bedroom as soon as he got back from school. It was clear that her son had no conceivable creative outlet to dedicate his talents to. This would bleed into all of the other aspects of his life (social, mental, even physical), leaving a negative impact and causing him to struggle as he could not find happiness in his life.

For Mary, accepting that she could not "fix," her son was the first step in helping him heal and encouraging him in the right direction. Parents might get nervous at this story and attempt to identify the root cause of the issue, thinking that it is easily preventable. For Mary and Jake, this came out of the left field. Looking back now, Jake says that it was probably the result of puberty and growing up as a teenager in general that led to him shutting down and unable to motivate himself to pursue the things he loved.

And so, Mary would enrol Jake into an afterschool drama program and later on in the summers, drama camp. These would end up being the highlights of Jake's time in high school because it allowed him to make friends and dedicate his time and efforts into his talents. He grew as an individual, learning new social skills and life lessons through interacting with his peers. With Mary understanding that he was an individual who needed encouragement from an external source, she opened up a world of personality for her son, who grew more confident and developed a strong sense of self-assurance.

We see creativity manifest throughout various aspects of our lives. Establishing these values and qualities from an early age allows it to appear naturally later on in your children's lives when faced with various social situations that require quick thinking and ingenuity. A significant part of creativity is the leadership that it fosters because it can give your children the confidence they need in their convictions. The critical thing to be wary of is that leadership can manifest in several ways during these formative years. Like most things, it does not have a simple set of specifications that a person must adhere to become a good leader. Instead, nurturing qualities that force an individual to branch out and think differently is how we find the means of developing these qualities. Nurturing the leader in your children does not necessarily mean you are setting your child up to become the next leader of a country. Instead, you are equipping them with the life skills they need to survive and thrive. This can appear later when your children have families of their own and are responsible for their children.

In its way, leadership is a culmination of all of these essential skills to instil into your children. Parents might struggle with this for several reasons, the most common being a financial burden. Parents cannot always afford extracurricular activities or afterschool programs that are listed below to foster these good values in their children. Nevertheless, that is not to say that this cannot be practised within the household. For example, teaching your children responsibilities at home can translate into leadership qualities. The most common instance is in being the oldest sibling. While parents are away, the oldest sibling can be in charge of their younger siblings. If your child is an only child, giving them small leadership roles to look after home responsibilities like walking the dog or taking out the trash may sound simple. Still, it establishes a pattern of behaviour that will carry on for a lifetime.

Siblings are an excellent way to establish responsibility with your children. Siblings teach your children conflict management and critical thinking. One of the ideal ways to do so is by letting your children deal with their sibling quarrels by themselves and coming up with their appropriate solutions. Many parents find that sibling quarrels tend to work themselves out without them having to step in. Mary found this to be accurate, as well. With Jake being the younger child, he was always at odds with his older brother Mark. Jake constantly fought with Mark, and Mary noticed many the fights tended to be rooted in Jake's anti-social behaviour while Mark was outgoing, popular and an extrovert. This time, Mary decided to step in by having a conversation with each of her sons separately, explaining the situation and why they needed to resolve it. She found that her intervention helped immensely, with Mark developing more empathy for his brother's plights.

In contrast, Jake developed more confidence and found himself growing less jealous of his brother's successes. They were able to work out the issue together, with Mary knowing when to step in to help her kids out. This is crucial for the success of relationships between their siblings because it teaches them to mitigate their issues.

Hobbies play a significant role in developing your children but be sure to remember that grades, while essential, are not the end all be all for your child's development into an individual. These hobbies are gateways into raising companies' leaders or being good husbands later on in their adult lives. These good habits will ultimately play a crucial role in creating a decent and good human being. So whether you choose to go through the hobby route or foster these qualities at home, you are setting your child up for advancement by teaching them the skills they will need to do their best as human beings and individuals, especially later on in their lives. Ultimately, raising sons is about helping them discover their skills, passions and purpose in life. Parents can help them along the way by investing in their passions and teaching them to develop their strengths and work on their weaknesses, much like Mary and Jake did.

Another story I want to share is with Daniel, who struggled to find his passion. This might be your case, as well. Finding a passion may take some time as it may require some trial and error to find the best skills and tasks to suit your child's interests. If this happens, do not fret. Daniel found himself struggling to find a passion after trying numerous things from music to cooking, writing, singing...the list goes on and on. Fortunately for Daniel, his parents were incredibly supportive by continually enrolling him in new classes and being proactive about where he was thriving and where he simply was not. Daniel faced a lot of rejection and was eventually feeling incredibly unmotivated as he went along, finally dropping all of these new hobbies altogether. One day, during physical education class, he discovered a love and excitement for rugby. The rest, as they say, is history. Daniel and his parents took some giving up for his passion to come to him naturally. While he was unmotivated and feeling too discouraged from the previous classes and activities he had pursued, to say that they offered no value at all to his life would be a huge disservice. Daniel learnt a lot about himself during his quest to find his love for rugby. His passion for the sport sparked because he had known that he was more potent in sports and loved physical activity through previous experiences. That is to say; he learned a great deal about himself through taking all of the other classes that ended up being more educational than worthless, as many people might be more inclined to think.

Particularly for boys, creative development is often placed on the back burner because physical education, mathematics, and logic are deemed more acceptable for this gender. But as it has been reiterated, it lies within parents to recognize how this can impede their children's development. Placing them in boxes and labelling them and creating even more limitations only hinders them in the long run. Rather than raising boys to be masculine and encourage only "manly hobbies", instead nurture their interests above all else.

A note about toxic masculinity: this is a social expectation that has been imposed on boys for centuries. This essentially forces men into thinking that to be masculine, they must hide their emotions, be dominant, and have a strong physique. This imagery is extremely dangerous for young and impressionable teens as they are continually being bombarded with this idea of the "ideal man" through social media like Instagram. This pressure is counterproductive and can have a profoundly negative impact on how men view their self-worth and in turn, view women and others around them. Having a conversation about toxic masculinity with your teen is an excellent way to educate your child about creating attainable goals that are realistic and beneficial for themselves and society. Toxic masculinity is why certain hobbies are frowned upon for males, and indeed why creativity is placed on the backburner when it comes to educating them.

The most important thing to remember here is that there are no hobbies catered explicitly to each gender. Thinking this way is merely ignorant, not to mention dated. Being in the 21st century, we celebrate the fact that there are no limits placed on boys or girls. Parents are responsible for showing their children that hard work and discipline will take them far in life, regardless of their interests. The essential thing is that they are safe, enjoying what they are doing and continuously learning.

Self-improvement is vital in raising your children. Helping them see that humans are blank canvases that need to be taught and constantly evolving is part of our responsibilities as a parent. Raising secure children is a daunting task, to do so, parents have to foster these skills that value growth and evolution as an individual so that your teens are not stagnant in their lives. This means that we have to encourage children to be productive with their time and nurture their free time by enrolling them in activities and hobbies that will further nourish their brains and teach them new things. Children are new to the world, which is why the responsibility weighs so heavily on parents to give their children daily instruction at first before allowing them to go off independently and make their own decisions.

So the next time you are exploring enrolling your child in an afterschool activity or new hobby, view all of the factors that will positively impact them because their childhood years are the perfect time to be trying new things.

The following is a list of often-overlooked hobbies for boys or deemed "too girly". These are great activities to encourage your child's development.

1. Theatre

Theatre is an incredible platform to get your children to develop their self-confidence and public speaking skills. Acting or even musical theatre can help uncover some untapped potential your teen may have. Theatre is also a social environment that many children thrive in. They are exposed to a cohort who provide support and friendship—exposing your teen boys to new ways of communicating and is an effective and safe space to serve as an emotional outlet. Theatre is an excellent way to foster cooperation and another facet of responsibilities that your child may not necessarily have at home. It is another way to be a part of an often overlooked team, for "teams" usually entails participating in sports. However, theatre is another way to encourage experimentation and going out of their comfort zone while still in a group setting.

2. Stand-up comedy

Teenagerhood is a great time to foster this hobby. Not only does it encourage writing skills and independent thinking, but it also places your teen in front of an audience. It's an excellent outlet for practising communicative skills and a place to expel emotions in a way that gives them the satisfaction and immediate gratification of an audience. It is also a place where criticism is given freely, so it helps your teens grow a thicker skin and understand implementing changes and tweaking their routines to be better than the last. By the time your kids are teenagers, it helps them develop a stronger sense of self that they will take with them well into adulthood. Having confidence is hugely valued and even taken for granted. Confidence is the key to overcoming a lot of social and personal anxieties that tend to plague teens. Finding ways to help your children realize their potential from a young age sets them up for the rest of their lifetime. While this hobby can seem out of the box, several drama schools and schools, in general, may feature courses or programs that you can enrol your children in to teach them the fundamentals of comedy for them to expand on.

3. Vlogging

The internet provides an infinite resource for your teen to develop themselves. Many teens have found success on YouTube as vloggers. By sharing their daily lives and their journeys, teens can communicate and understand an audience. Teens can also find their niche of what they may want to share and develop their video format ideas. This can teach them a slew of other skills from video editing to business management should they become successful, and their popularity grows. It also encourages responsibility as your teens will have an audience to respond to.

4. Pottery

Pottery enables your teen to get to use their cognitive and tactile skills to produce creations. Through pottery, they can engage in a process that can help them concentrate and focus. Pottery is a quiet activity that can allow your teen time to destress and relax while also spending their time productively.

5. Dancing

There is bound to be one that your teen son will enjoy with so many dance styles that exist. Dancing is especially beneficial because it gives your child another vantage point to understanding culture and learns about traditions and customs. It opens them to the world around them and its diversities and leads to empathy and respect for the differences around us. It also gives your teenage sons the physical activity they may not be regularly getting as they practice every day.

6. Skating

Whether your teen son chooses to skate professionally, competitively, or recreationally, this is another way to get him moving and getting physical activity. It allows them to focus and express themselves through their body and movement. It promotes blood circulation and flexibility, things that are often overlooked for teens who are glued to their computer monitors always. Rather than being a violent sport, it encourages strength gracefully. Don't be fooled by how professionals make skating seem so effortless; it requires plenty of strength and discipline.

7. Gardening

This hobby is an excellent way to get your teen boys outside and get in touch with their environment and nature. Learning about products and flowers broadens your child's knowledge and exposes them to the world that exists outside. Gardening also involves being a nurturer, which is often not emphasized for boys in the school curriculum or daily lives. It affords your teen son the responsibility of caring for another living thing while also allowing them to express their creativity by exploring the world beyond the confines of the inside.

8. Cooking

Similar to gardening, cooking is another way to foster creativity as your teen son learns their way around the kitchen and develops an understanding of fruits, vegetables, seasonings, and how they may all come together to create a final product that they can be proud of. This way, it also teaches sons that the kitchen is not a space that is exclusive to women only. Cooking is also an important life skill to have that your child should be prepared with as they grow and move on to the next stages of their lives.

9. Meditation/ Scripture reading

Meditation is a fantastic hobby to facilitate mental health in a positive and accepting environment. It's a great way to relax from the chaos of everyday life and to take a moment to breathe and focus on yourself, rather than everything going on around you. It also encourages self-reflection, which is always an excellent way to promote positive thinking.

David found a secret which he shared to help all young people in the book of

Psalm 119:9-11

> How can young people keep their lives pure?
>
> By obeying your commands.
>
> [10] With all my heart I try to serve you;
>
> Keep me from disobeying your commandments.
>
> [11] I keep your law in my heart,
>
> So that I will not sin against you.

I John 2:14 says the same "I have written to you, young men,

> because you are strong,
>
> the word of God abides in you,

and you have overcome the evil one." Keeping the word of God and obeying the instructions makes young people have inner strength.

Singing

Teen boys are often overlooked when it comes to pursuing singing. There are plenty of singing styles that will appeal to your son and their preferences and pique their interest. Many boys sing before puberty but feel the need to stop once their voices have changed. This certainly does not have to be the case. Through singing, they can explore music interests and develop a deeper understanding of the procedure and another facet of the experience.

These hobbies have been featured here, mostly because of the stigma surrounding them for teen boys who fear pursuing these hobbies. Your kids may feel resistant to pursuing these hobbies, which is an excellent opportunity to discuss why and talk about the inherent biases in our minds. Take the chance to explain to your teen boys that there is nothing wrong with pursuing these hobbies, especially if they already have an interest in them and want to continue them but are afraid of criticism. Being a source of support and reassurance for your teen boys helps them build confidence and encourages them to pursue their interests wholeheartedly and dedicatedly.

Additionally, specific skills are often overlooked when raising boys as parents stick to stereotypes and adhere to gender roles and the so-called duties of each gender. This ends up setting your son up for failure as they will be unprepared for survival in the real world. There are some skills that many men are unfamiliar with because they were coddled and taught that they were the job of women.

- Basic household chores: both sons and daughters must have an understanding of how to run a household. Assigning housework and duties is not limited to women only. Doing dishes, laundry and other necessary chores teach sons to have essential cleanliness and responsibility for their environment.

- Basic cooking: being able to cook is a means of survival. Parents tend to assume that sons are simply disinterested in cooking, and again, this can be a vast generalization. Teaching them the basics is a way to prepare them for when they move out it gives them the ability to be more self-sufficient.

- Understanding the female body: plenty of men are still unsure how the female body works, especially with periods, PMS, and even pregnancy. While you don't have to get down to the nitty-gritty of details, having a basic understanding of biology will help your sons better understand the world in general. Plenty of males avoid this education because it is deemed to be not in their realm, but it is equally important to understand these things as it is to understand their biological processes.

Chapter 3:
Handling Anger as a Parent

D isciplining older children can be difficult for parents to face because it can be more complex than disciplining younger children. Because your children are older now, they expect an increased amount of independence and discipline from parents simply does

not fall into that category. Many teens see their parents' discipline as a form of control or overly strict and not trusting them with the freedom they think they might have deserved. So, when it comes down to it, your disciplining techniques might be met with reluctance and even rebellion. Teens will continuously test your patience and the limits of their independence while attempting to strike a balance as they enter this new stage of adolescence.

As they experience new and extreme emotions from physical, emotional, and social changes through puberty and ageing, this time can be tumultuous. This is where you as the parent enter to help adolescents grapple with these big changes, and sometimes it might mean disciplining them and taking away their privileges for them to learn that there are consequences to their actions. Particularly during these formative years, severe mental health issues can emerge at this time. Most commonly, we see depression and anxiety manifesting as your teen goes to school and is faced with social interactions that can be negative. Deteriorating mental health can be attributed to many things, and there never is a straightforward answer because it is so complex and challenging to come to terms with.

The techniques you use may take some getting used to as every teen is different and grows up in varying environments. Ultimately, it lies on you to know your child and distinguish what will and will not be best for them, especially in imparting lessons. Adolescence is the time for parents to relinquish their reins on guiding their children and strike a good balance between giving them freedom while still teaching them through life. For many teens, this means less supervision, later curfews, or merely arguing with the decisions you may have made for them. Teens want to do things in their way and at their own time and n0t being told what to do by authoritative figures like their parents or teachers is the antithesis to this. Teenagerhood also means breaking the rules. Your teens may disagree with your decision not to allow them to go to outings and may sneak out or lie to get out of your rules, but it does not have to be this way.

From a parents' point of view, this time is challenging because it may seem like your child is doing everything in their power to test you and frustrate you. Teens will continuously push the envelope when it comes to rules and regulations, and for you, the best way to grapple with this is to remember that they will grow out of this phase. Stay calm and always remember to never act out of anger. As always, children are wired to mimic others, and extreme responses like anger when you're frustrated can reflect in your children as well. That is not to say that you are not allowed to be angry. But managing your anger, frustration, and stress healthily is crucial for both you and your children.

The following are some tips for parents to manage anger or frustration healthily:

1. Breathe

Taking a few moments to pause and breathe to process the situation. This is extremely important because it allows you to think things through; like how the situation may have escalated and how to bring it back to the civil and respectful point. But before you even begin to try and put pieces together in a situation that your child is involved in, take a second to breathe in and out and count silently to ten. Getting into the right framework is important to think things through logically.

   1. "This too, shall pass."

Your children did not stay in their terrible twos forever. Likewise, this teenage rebellion will also eventually phase out, provided that you are supplying them with the right consequences and imparting them with lessons that they need to learn. To grow out of this phase and for this time of backtalking and disrespect to stop, you have to nip it in the bud early-on so that your teens can decipher right from wrong in terms of appropriate and acceptable behaviours and attitudes. Failure to do so will result in meltdowns in adulthood that are most definitely inexcusable and out of the question for acceptable adult behaviours.

3. Step away

Parents often send their children to their bedrooms to reflect on their poor behaviour before talking with them. This strategy works because not only do kids get a chance at self-reflection but so do adults. This is the time to think about what punishment your child will receive and the conversation that needs to be heard about curbing poor behaviour or attitudes.

4. Control your anger

Anger can often lead us to do things we might regret immediately. Rather than acting out of anger, approach your anger critically, and try to think rationally. Sometimes your children may act in an aggravating and frustrating way that may warrant getting angry, especially if they endanger themselves or do things you have explicitly told them not to do. However, in some cases, anger can form irrationally when your children do not deserve it. Rather than immediately acting on the offence that creates, consider why exactly you feel this way. For example, sometimes you might be taking your anger out on your kid after a long and stressful day at work. Your child is not your emotional punching bag, so always be wary of how you are responding to your emotions. "I told you" is wrong to tell teenagers when they have done things wrong, even if you have told them. The best way to go about the damage is just to start looking for solutions and avoid the use of the phrase "I told you."

5. Avoid physical punishment

Spanking and slapping your children never teach them anything constructive, aside from making them fear you. Hitting your children can profoundly negatively impact your child's development that can last throughout their lives. Being hurt by a parent destroys trust and a strong foundational basis. So while you may feel angry and frustrated, the answer is never to spank your children in your rage. It can render all of the positive things you have done as a parent completely useless because your child will grow to fear your punishment and find ways to work around it.

6. Assert authority

While your children should not fear you, they should respect you as an authoritative figure in their lives. Reacting out of anger can often inspire unreasonable threats, which will in turn, undermine your authority. Rather than immediately punishing them with threats that will not be followed through, take some time to think about an appropriate punishment that will make them learn and understand why they are being punished in the first place.

Chapter 4:
Methods to Discipline Teen Boys

Once you have recognized that you are in a situation where your child will have to be disciplined, parents are often unsure of how to go about actually disciplining their teen boys. While these techniques are interchangeable and appropriate to be used on your teen girls as well, here are some actions for you to employ:

1. Remove electronics

Screen time is essential to most teenagers, with their cell phones, laptops, and TVs being readily available. In particular, cell phones are crucial for a teen's social life, with social media being a source of entertainment and fun. Restricting these privileges can get your message across to your teenager. By placing time limits, your teens will be compelled to reflect on their behaviour and encouraged to rethink their attitudes for the next time.

2. Restrict time with friends

Misbehaviour can manifest in many forms, and sometimes your children may not be acting alone. You absolutely can take away their right to see their friends for a while. By restricting them for a few days or cancelling a plan they might have had as a consequence, this will serve as a reminder for them to make better choices next time.

3. Tighten the rules

When your teen knowingly violates the rules you have laid out, this may be a way for them to convey that they cannot handle the new freedoms and independence that teenagerhood may bring. Giving them an earlier curfew might curb some of their inability to handle the newfound freedom that brings about recklessness and rebellion. Consider tightening the rules and changing them up to suit your child's development better.

4. Not all consequences will be imparted by you

Natural consequences can occur from certain situations, and they can provide an even better learning lesson for your kids. But it's essential to make sure the natural results will teach your teen something vital that they will hold onto. This is your chance to let your children be independent and allow them to face the natural consequences that occur from their actions. For example, teens quickly understand that forgoing their homework and studying will impede their chances of getting into a good college or university. Some choose to test this and push the envelope by neglecting these responsibilities.

The natural consequence of this is that they will face a difficult time when it comes to applying to college because their grades are simply not up to par. As much as you want your children to succeed, sometimes they need to experience the consequences of taking their responsibilities seriously.

5. Provide logical consequences

Invent consequences that are directly tied to the poor decisions your teen chose to make. As they are older and feel more inclined to make their own decisions, creating consequences also benefits from preparing them for what is to come as they enter adulthood. For example, if your teen breaks something of value deliberately, make them pay to fix it. Or, if they are irresponsible with driving and the car, take away their driving privileges. These are logical and realistic consequences that will happen in the real world as well. They are not just limited to the household.

6. Assign extra responsibilities

Sometimes children need to earn back the privileges they may have gotten in the process of maturing. Take away their privileges and assign extra work for them to complete, like chores or helping out around the house to earn back the trust they have broken.

7. Be consistent

Mean what you say when you decide to discipline your child. Make the right decision on the best course of action, and the critical part is to stick with it, no matter how angry or upset your teen may be getting. Setting a pattern of consequences to your teen's poor behaviour and attitude will get through to them that all actions have immediate results that they will have to face.

8. Know your teen

Understand your teen's personality to figure out the healthiest and most effective consequences for your teens. Knowing what they are motivated by and the privileges that they treasure is a great place to start to determine the best course of action. This means that you must foster a strong relationship with them with open communication lines and judgment-free conversations. This is your chance to be more of a friend to your child as they divulge their details and share the things that may be bothering them or weighing down on them. Or on the flip side, they may tell you about the areas that they are thriving in. Mentally catalogue these things and keep up with the changes in their lives, unlike friends that come and go as these facts will come in handy when trying to parent your children.

9. Walk away

If you find that your teen is being disrespectful towards you and saying things that are extremely hurtful or overly argumentative, sometimes one of the best ways to curb this is simply to walk away. You may choose to say something like "Until you can speak to me like an adult, I won't be having this conversation with you." Then follow up with a privilege being taken away. This way, your child will have no one to argue with and will be forced to re-evaluate how they speak to you to regain their consequences. This is also the time to talk to them about how they externalize their anger. Speaking rudely to a parent is never the way for them to get their point across.

Disciplining your children can be a stressful and complicated aspect of raising kids that many parents dread but the reality is that it is necessary to teach them the appropriate way of life. Employ these tactics to try and teach them why good behaviour and attitudes in responding to the various situations that will arise in their lifetime. Teaching children to cope and manage from a young age is a valuable skill to have as it will follow them well into adulthood. While these consequences might seem exclusive to the parent and child dynamic, many parallels can be drawn when your children enter the real world.

Chapter 5: Creating A Good Environment to Raise Teens

As much as punishments are essential for their development, there is a slew of other aspects that are also important to focus on when it comes to raising happy and healthy teenagers.

Focus on the positives to foster an encouraging environment for your teens. For adolescents, they are just trying to figure things out at their own pace and time. Parents and teachers encourage teens because they have experience in how the real world works and the world will not always tilt to their will or pace. As much as your child will make mistakes and test their boundaries, continually being on their case and punishing them for every mistake, they make sometimes might be a counterproductive approach. Instead, encourage and praise them by placing emphasis on the positive actions and why they were positive.

Set clear expectations for your teens to follow. Having wild and elaborate schemes only set them up for failure. With so many authoritative figures and rules to remember, the rules you set must be clear and concise so that your teens will see what is important to you. This is also a way to set them up to follow your rules if they are fair and straightforward. For example, expecting to be treated respectfully is a golden rule and a basic expectation that every child must be accustomed to. Communicate your expectations effectively and talk to your children about your feelings and desires. Let your teen son know what you expect from him and always explain why they understand your logic. For example, let your teens know that A's and B's are acceptable grades for you because anything lower will hinder their route to college. Or make completion of homework a prerequisite before they hang out with their friends. Consider putting your expectations in writing, email, or text it to him. This way, children will not be able to forget them as there will be a constant reminder.

Get and draw your teenagers to open up to you by avoiding "yes" or "no" answers. Instead, talk to them about where they are thriving in school and where they may be struggling. Rather than criticizing them for doing poorly, this is a chance to develop a plan to move forward to be successful on their next test on the exam. To establish a strong relationship with your teens as they spend an increasing amount of time away from home, regularly ask them how their education is going, who their new friends are. And how their quiet times, study time, extracurricular activities might be going. Setting time aside to talk to them about how things will help your teens grapple with the complex emotions they might be experiencing.

Whatever your household expectations are about relationships, this is the time to show your support for your children by encouraging them to discuss their lives. Parents find this aspect of their teens growing up incredibly uncomfortable, but it is usually better than for you to have assumptions about your teen, rather than not. This way, you can prepare them for what is out there and warn them about the dangers that exist.

Validate your children's' feelings by being an active listener. As much as communicating with them is important, listening is equally essential to be a good source of support for your kids. Offer them feedback and try to provide them with advice if they ask you for it. Validate how they are feeling and be specific when you acknowledge their feelings. It helps teens feel heard and understood because this period in their life being so volatile and complicated.

One of the enormous challenges parents face during this time is learning when to let go of their children and give them the independence they need to thrive and find their place in the world. The teenage years are crucial for this very reason. Not relinquishing control over your children can lead to disastrous effects as adolescents and parents will become at odds. Children will resent their parents for their overcontrolling nature, while parents will continue to face frustration and disappointment because their child refuses to listen to them.

Finding that balance is the biggest tip that can be taken away from this book—understanding where your child thrives and where they fall short is how to build the foundational blocks to help them developmentally and socially. For parents, this is the biggest challenge because they seek to be a friend to their children while also being an authoritative figure that they respect.

When your children are young, you dictate every aspect of their lives; from what time they eat, what time they sleep, what they watch, etc. Teens are the exact opposite of this as they immediately feel able to handle the responsibilities that adulthood may bring and experience a surge of confidence in transitioning from the adolescent age group. This is the time where adolescents feel like they can control their destiny and make their own decisions.

Teenagerhood is a time for parents to recognize that this is where they need to allow their children to flourish independently. When kids reach adolescence, they need to prepare for adulthood on their terms, and parents have to foster this need to be independent to flourish. Attempting to dictate their lives by your schedule every day and controlling every part of their lives will eventually lead to them defying you the first chance they get and finding ways around your punishments and consequences.

This by no means entails that this is the parent's chance to relax and completely release their teens' attention or time. While parents are not the immediate influence on their children anymore, they still play a massive aspect in their lives as a constant source of stability and comfort as they are involved in their child's life. By shifting our focus onto our teens and letting them dictate the course of their lives, this means that your children will get a chance to make mistakes and learn some real-life lessons that need to be taught and not necessarily by you. Your job here is to provide them with the guidance and emotional support they need to overcome the challenges life presents.

Raising teenagers is not an easy thing because your kids will argue and have a differing view from you. Parents often feel helpless when they have especially argumentative kids as they feel like they're only not getting through to them. But ultimately, it is how you deal with these difficult times with your children that will have the most significant impact on them and will stay with them for the rest of their lives, so never rush when it comes to disciplining your children. Your influence now has to evolve along with your kids. Because they have this inherent need to be independent, merely telling them what to do can lead to even more arguments and strife between the parent and child dynamic. Some parents take this time to treat their children as adults instead of respecting their choices and finding the balance needed where you are still an authoritative figure that they seek guidance from. Talk to them like you would with other adults and do not sugar-coat things. Teens want to know they are in control of the situation, rather than feel lesser than and unable to make decisions for themselves.

As soon as puberty hits, a string of uncertainties and new developments will arise that your children might not respond well to. They may attempt to deal with changes personally and privately. Still, sometimes they may yearn for support from their parents to navigate through whatever they may be going through, whether mentally, physically, or socially. To provide the support that your child needs, you will have to discuss uncomfortable topics with them. This can be a too daunting task, but it is incredibly crucial to support your teens, especially boys. Boys are more often than not encouraged to keep their personal feelings and emotions bottled up than their female counterparts.

Featured below is a condensed list of important subjects to broach with your children, regardless of gender.

- Mental health: Prioritize your child's mental health just as you prioritize their physical health. Boys are often told to bottle up their feelings and to curb this, start by having discussions about their feelings and what they may be experiencing. This is a way to show them that their feelings are valued and allowed. It also presents to them that you care for their mental wellbeing.

- Sexual activity: Teen years means engaging in relationships that can lead to sexual activity. While schools provide health education, make sure to reiterate to your teens with the talk. Be open and blunt with your teens about the dangers and temptations.

- Alcohol and drugs: Be open and blunt with your teens about the dangers and temptations of alcohol and drugs. You want to trust them to make the right decisions if they are ever faced with substances, especially when underage. Educating them on the dangers that these substances pose is incredibly crucial to making sure that they are well-informed when faced with challenging situations.

- Internet safety: Social media and the internet are a huge part of most teenagers' lives. It plays a massive impact on moulding adolescence, and teens can often get so caught up on the latest internet trends. Impart on them safe procedures online, like withholding personal information and protecting their identity. Furthermore, It is important to reiterate that social media is too superficial. Social media can harm your child's self-esteem and confidence, so having a healthy relationship with Instagram, Facebook, and Twitter are essential to develop.

- Saying 'no': The word no is reiterated enough for teens. Educate your children on potential uncomfortable and dangerous threats that exist out in the world and provide them with a way out by letting them know that should they ever be in an awkward situation, you will always be there to support them and help them.

Conversation with teenage boys

With limited returns, contact with teenage boys always takes a significant effort. The monosyllable answers like ok.. no.. yeah.. dunno, whatever will frustrate the calmest parents. Those basic (non) answers will lead to further questions escalating to open up or offer more information to the boy. With a burst of hostility/anger, the teenager's system will react. With an expression of disdain or an audible tone of fear, they will counter.

An adolescent boy will engage in a whirlwind of extensive conversation on a matter of concern, amid the occasional lack of communication. Only pay attention. When they open up, don't discount them or ignore them. Otherwise, you will lose your reputation.

The Moms

When it comes to contact with a teenage child, less is better. A well-enunciated grunt may take the position of a long sentence. Mums need to know that attempting to describe things in depth is wasting their mental resources. An adolescent boy can hear just five or ten words. They shut down after that. Cut all correspondence down to one or two words, or even fewer mothers!

The Father

To be a role model, teenage boys need a strong adult guy. Because of the loss of a parent in a boy's life, several youth harm reports exist. The human male has software that requires them to transform a child into an adult. This usually entails a passage rite set up by other adult males. For this rite of passage, a tutor, such as a father, may train the teenager. Much differently from most of the modern experience, our present world is made up. This programming does, however, still exist. Today, we are not handling this programming need sufficiently, which adds to today's social challenges.

Dad, Fathers or male role models need to walk their talk. Dads, first get your act together. Male role models need to pass on and show not tell, their knowledge of relationships, income, jobs, company, life, etc. Boys learn by doing rather than talking. Dads, making your sons understand how to be a guy is your responsibility.

Having a father who is worthy of emulation can set the life of a teenage boy straight. He will look forward to living a replica life of his father.

Physical Task

Most teenage boys need to stay engaged. Testosterone expenditure and socialization would be allowed through participating in a sport or other physical activity. Boys want to be aggressive and challenge each other physically. Think about puppies or bear cubs. Playing fighting is a big part of their creation among teenage male animals.

Be alright with pressing and shoving people. Dads, let your son test you physically with boxing, football, mountain biking, etc. Don't just let them win," but balance their skill instead. Continual loss is going to be discouraging. They will deservedly defeat you at some point. A significant bonding tool for parents is adequate and regular physical interaction.

With their son, moms may also participate in physical activity. It is also okay to give a friendly bump to their sons while passing or a gentle punch. A welcome physical touch from any parent may be a back scratch or massage. Let them sense your presence.

For several boys, sitting in a chair is a struggle. There is a story about a teacher who taught his son to recite the verses while taking them on a jog to his male pupil, the Talmud. As they study, let them run. Maybe when on an exercise bike, they can read. This was a method used to engage his son's thinking while also participating in physical activity. While you may be inclined to feel discouraged that your son cannot pay attention quietly for long periods, choose to instead turn this into a positive by using it to everyone's advantage. In this case, the teacher decided to take his pupil's abilities and better his lessons that benefited both teacher and student. It ensured a more engaged pupil and a teacher who had a more pleasant time teaching.

Be Robust

Teenage boys will send out a torrent of nasty words in the face of a father, considering the frequent lack of communication skills. They'll appear to dislike you for a moment, and then wonder if the next moment is for dinner. They're not intimate, they're all hormones. Come on, mothers; you know that you can relate to a case like that.

Be Competent

Bear in mind that the adolescent years are also a time of research. Experimentation often entails dangerous activities. They can refrain from using sex, narcotics, beer, and tobacco. Before they have ample exposure to them, explore these topics freely with your son. This will raise the likelihood that when the time comes where they are faced with deciding on whether to consume alcohol or take drugs, they will behave responsibly. Establishing these ideals early on is not difficult. Parents often encounter problems because they have made these subjects taboo in the household. But the key is to establish open communication lines between everyone to instil the values you want your sons to emulate early on. If you teach your children from a young age that drugs are harmful, they will feel a stronger sense of responsibility because they can see the logic and reasoning behind these ideals. For your teenage boy, share family values and chat about what you think is right and wrong.

Have an attempt to consider your child's peers and the parents of their friends. Parent-to-parent contact can help create a healthy atmosphere for teens. Parents should help each other keep track of their teens' actions, without directing their activities individually to make them behave like little kids.

Pleasant and Humor

Teenage boys enjoy laughing and having fun. To adults, the comedy could sound juvenile—well, it is. Let them be dumb. Whatever you hear teenage boys laugh at, you may cringe. Give them a brief reminder and move on to suitability.

Bear in mind that a hearty laugh may be a fitting solution to the unconscious response of a youth to a challenge from an adult. It doesn't always take a serious and dramatic reaction to let them know their negative reaction. A pleasant tickle and a joke can help quell bad feelings sometimes.

Put yourself in their position

Pause to wonder where they are coming from as things start to go off course. Bear in mind that they have multiple thoughts, views, fears, wishes, etc. They will see the case differently than you will. Before things pass to the next step, get their insight. You may want them to wear new clothes. Be open to the truth of them having motivations of their own for wearing anything different. Stand your ground after you have listened to them. Be open to an agreement if the case permits versatility.

Choose Your Fights

Parents and teenage boys are going to butt heads. Differentiating between critical concerns and minor issues is crucial. Urgent situations are those that would have a significant effect on your son or family. Minor complications are those that can present a temporary setback. Be firm on the critical problems and agile on the minor issues.

Talk it out when there is a disagreement. Get their own opinion. Share your view. Clarify all the pros and the cons. In other words, treat them while addressing the dilemma like an adult. When making a decision, be a dad.

Set prospects

Children, in general, ought to have limits set. Teens, where there is opposition, would be able to have a more detailed statement. There is an intuition behind the opposition if the expectations are rational.

It is necessary to have them engage in the development of aspirations as teenage adults. Open dialogue and get their input on setting school grade criteria, actions, activities, etc. They are more likely to obey them as they help set the rules. Your teenage boy might believe he is on his own without fair expectations or you do not care as a father.

They will be vulnerable without this simple understanding of what to expect and will try to challenge you to see where in their world the actual limits are found. They ought to know who is in charge, what the rules are, and the repercussions of disobeying boys' rules to be happy.

Value the Dignity of Your Teenage Boy

It can be challenging for individual parents to embrace the idea of privacy for their children because they believe their company is everything their children do have. However, allowing some anonymity is crucial to making your teenage boy become an adolescent adult. If vital warning signs of trouble remain, then violating the privacy of your child is appropriate. Otherwise, backing off is a smart idea.

This suggests that your teenager's space, messages, e-mails, and phone calls should be confidential (Depending on the relationship built). Please don't presume that your son will share with you all his feelings or hobbies. Enable your son to place you on his friend's list for social media such as Facebook. This encourages parents to see what they're posting and doing to everyone in general.

For safety purposes, of course, you should still know where teenagers are heading, when they're going to come back, what they're doing, and with whom. Keep it general, not every aspect of their operation needs to be learned. The order would generate only resistance.

Hold Your Confidence

The teenage years, by extension, are just seven years long, between 13 and 19. You survived an infant crying through the night as a mom, the miserable twos, potty training, school, and another seven or so years of everyday trials and tribulations of infancy. Raising an adolescent can feel like a setback to your previous expertise in parenting. Instead, it is a test of your talents in adult school. You should not regard your teenage boy as a girl. Become his coach for adulthood, instead.

Chapter 6:
A Parent's Survival Guide to Teenage Boys

When their' tweener' grows a foot taller and becomes uncommunicative and often explosive, parents are sometimes astonished. Welcome to a teenage boy's world.

Parents need to realize that through their progression to adulthood, this is a normal process boy go through. A fascinating, but the explosive combination is produced by the mix of testosterone running through their bloodstream and a natural desire to differentiate from their parents.

You look at your son, and you ask him to do a job. In a rage, he cries out. His poor language abilities stop him from being able to communicate his thoughts or describe them. You take this reaction as a personal assault and some kind of flaw in your son. Take a look back and slowly breathe. This condition has arisen since there were teenage boys on the first day.

The teenage boy is seen stereotypically as a wild, rebellious adolescent who is frequently in conflict with his parents.

Although adolescent boys have their emotional ups and downs, they have a practical and compassionate side.

Developing freedom is the main force for adolescents. Informs that would frustrate kin, this is embodied. A boy who usually conforms to his parents' wishes will unexpectedly show himself and share his views. They strongly protest against the control of their parents and establish a moral code of their own.

Parents need to step back to realize that they need to build and create their own lives for teens (boys and girls). Do you listen to your adolescents as their feelings and ideas are expressed? Do you make it easy for them to have differing views and thoughts than yours? As you will for every other human, you ought to respect their opinions and viewpoints. For harmful or destructive wishes/thoughts, sound parental decision and interference are, of course, to be required.

Handling Teenage Boys

Parenting is demanding. None of the schools teaches how to rear children, nor do we have life models to follow. Otherwise, we will not have grandparents who spoil our teens because they believe they were not successful parents and so by their grand teenagers, would like to correct their errors; oblivious of our thoughts that they are overdoing it. Often the generational contrast of today from past generations makes it difficult to follow examples of life.

There is no question about it, and it can be challenging to raise teenagers; in reality, coping with teenagers is a feat with two parents, and dealing with teenagers is a struggle with only the wife. Regardless of how the single mother ended up becoming a single mother - death, divorce, and abandonment - she still has to play the father's role.

Plenty of parents, due to several circumstances, have had to become single parents out of necessity. Handling boys when you are a single parent and juggling all life stressors can be extremely challenging. Single parenting takes a considerable amount of courage and resourcefulness to play both roles of mother and father. The responsibilities are upped by a tenfold on the parent. Parenting can often be a thankless job that frustrates parents to no end. But at the same time, it can be an enriching experience to rear children.

For single parents, like most things, there is no one-stop-shop for raising children. It requires a tremendous amount of resilience and strength to face the journey of parenthood as an individual.

Maya is a single parent of three boys. The difficulties she faced were immense as she tried to figure out how to parent three sons while juggling her career and making ends meet. The most important tip that propelled her household into an organized space with all family members thriving was setting clear guidelines for behavioural standards. Maya understood that her sons were growing increasingly independent every day as they reached their teen years and saw that they needed guidance when facing crucial challenges that would impact their lives. For Maya, finding that balance was the most challenging part about being a single parent. But at the same time, it was not impossible. This took a lot of trial and error for her household to be as successful as it is today.

Furthermore, she involved her children in the major decisions that would impact the house. This is crucial. Because your children are young, do not underestimate their opinions and treat them with the respect they deserve.

A crucial aspect of Maya's journey in parenthood with her three sons made her realize that there is no one size fits all approach to parenting. Every family is completely different, and no two circumstances can be the same. By accepting this, she could cater to parenting and manage her household to best suit her family. There is no quick-fix approach, or generic advice is available for how to treat your adolescents. To resolve the challenging challenge, any scenario needs a clear recommendation. But to help you navigate your teens, we will take those simple steps:

1. Set Laws

Your teens need to know the laws of your house and the repercussions of not adopting them. Make sure you negotiate this with them before deciding the rules and make adjustments if very necessary. You need to get their opinion on the laws that you want to follow. They are expected to have a buy-in to the rules. If possible, an understanding or majority must prevail.

2. Don't be too indulgent.

Do not be lenient now that you have a consensus. Laws are not produced to be ignored. They must accept the repercussions if they refuse to comply with your rules.

3. Give your teenagers period.

Financial difficulties are one of the significant obstacles of most single moms. While you are very concerned about earning a living for your families, you must not do away with time for your teens. During dinner, you will still find time to ask them about their day. This, in truth, is one of the rules you have to make. At a particular moment, the teens must be home, and you must share dinner.

4. Chat about crucial challenges for them.

Do not be ashamed to talk about drugs or underage sex. Your youth need to realize that in our culture you are mindful of these urgent challenges and that the goal is for them to resist temptations and social influences that will drive them to make the decision they will regret in the future.

5. Be careful of their mates

Guide them to select a good company. To know their peers and to make friends with their coworkers. You'd know who to call if complications arose. If your teens become secretive, you might even get details from their peers.

A story I would like to share features three brothers living together with their single mother, Janice. As a single parent, Janice figured out parenting her three sons through trial and error and found that the best way to motivate and discipline them was through a star system. The three brothers experienced difficulty for years, but as they aged, they developed endurance and perseverance. More importantly, Janice was able to impart a strong sense of independence within each of her sons that reflected in their habits as they were diligent and disciplined in cleaning up after themselves and following through with the roles they were designated within the household. Janice's star system entailed an inspection in their rooms and making sure they completed all of their tasks every week by Saturday morning, which awarded them a star sticker. Their duties included things like tidying their room, cleaning their clothes and shoes and helping her maintain a clean and tidy house. These stickers culminated to a prize by the end of the year.

On one particular inspection, Janice caught drink bottles underneath one of the brothers' beds. She scolded the boys for leaving a mess under their beds and compromising the standard they had held to a high regard for so long. She was reminded of a period when the boys realized the team effort that had to go into following all of the responsibilities and duties that were assigned to each of them individually. This was one of the biggest lessons that taught her sons to tolerate each other, persevere, and show each other patience as everything was a collective group effort. As all three sons shared a bedroom for their whole lives, they were all equally responsible for the messes they made. These skills and values they learned could not have been fully actualized if they had slept in separate rooms their whole lives. Sharing a room helped each of them learn how to look after themselves. The oldest brother exemplified the behaviour that was expected, which the younger siblings followed.

When parents and teachers understand a teen's point of view, this dramatically encourages them positively. The youngest son started to change when he had Miss Helen as his English teacher. She became a positive figurehead in his life as she empowered him with her words of praise. She maintained a strong connection with him by deliberately investing in his interests. This grew an understanding for him as an individual, rather than other teachers at school merely seeing him as another student among a sea of many more. Miss Helen believed in him and his abilities, which completely changed his outlook. He conveyed to her that he was not lazy, but unmotivated because he was never in the right group of friends. She was able to see that certain activities bored him and made adjustments that suited him. Being an attentive and understanding teacher was one of the highlights of his education during this time.

The moral here is that parents and teachers can be huge role models for their kids and students. Adults have a significant impact on the way kids act and how they perceive themselves. It's up to adults to understand kids at a deeper level and treat them as their individuals. Too often do adults cast aside children because they might not completely understand the nuances that adulthood brings. But the reality is that kids are incredibly wise and often understand more than they let on.

The same goes for teens. A lot of teenage angst is rooted in them not being treated with the respect they deserve. Teens often get cast aside as hormonal and too emotional to be able to handle adult subjects. But this is far from the truth. Teens are far more knowledgeable than many people want to believe. Often, teens are perhaps more knowledgeable about the goings-on in the world than adults. The moral here is to take the time to get to know your teens on an individual level. Never allow them to stray isolated for too long because they may be struggling with something on a deeper level. Even if they are not struggling, seeing that they have a constant support system is sometimes very much needed.

With teenage self-esteem and enhancing their confidence. For teens, there are numerous and varied challenges, but taking the issue of self-esteem first.

About adolescents! Teenagers are trapped in an in-between environment. They're neither children nor grown-ups. They respond to physical and behavioural changes, including emotional extremes triggered in the brain's emotion-regulating portion by extra stimulation. AND hormones!

Needless to say, this is on the problem list for teens right up there! For many teenagers, this is a frustrating moment!

This time is hugely confusing for teenagers as they are met with new developments and are faced with their hormones changing. This can be extremely disturbing for parents, especially if they are unprepared to face their teens' unique attitude and behavioural changes.

This is mostly a time when parents might feel like they have lost control over their teens. You may feel like your role as a parent is redundant because your teens are acting increasingly like an adult. To put it simply, you may feel like your kids do not need you anymore. But because your teens are undergoing newfound independence and maturity into their young adult years, this can be a complicated thing for them to navigate alone, which is why it is so immensely crucial for parents to reiterate their role.

Losing control over your teens might come in some forms. You may feel like they are not listening to you or shutting you out of their lives. Your relationship with them might be hanging by a thread because they refuse to turn to you. This loss of control can be alarming for most parents.

Depending on the severity of the situation, you can do a few things to cope with this and try to fix the problem as quick as best as possible.

1. Find a neutral party. Something more significant might be affecting your teen deeply that they may not want to admit to you. Involving a neutral party that they trust like an aunt or uncle, teacher or seeking professional help from a therapist might be a route to pursue if you find that your attempts to reconnect with your child are not being met.
2. Be open with your teens and allow them to be honest without fear of consequences or punishment. This is when they will make a lot of mistakes, so allow them to do so.
3. Discipline them like an adult. The punishments you may have used when they were younger might not

have the same effect as it would today. Be adaptable to their changes and act accordingly when you want to instil a lesson.

4. Rebuild respect. Sometimes resentment or anger might be festering, leading to your teen denying your role as the adult and the parent. If so, you might have to revisit your actions and reflect where you may have wronged your child in any way. This can be difficult to do, but very crucial if this is the case. In this instance, the goal is to rebuild respect between yourself and your teen so that they can grow to trust you once more.

5. Accept change. Sometimes you may feel like you are losing control over your teen, but the truth is that they are only growing up and experiencing the newfound privileges and perks of being older. The issue might not lay within your teen and instead be rooted in you not accepting the realities of change and evolution. If this is the case, you might have to reevaluate how you perceive your children because they are more than children and will soon become fully-fledged working members of society.

You may feel at this time that you are trying to rein in a wayward child, and all of the values and qualities you have attempted to instil over the years flying out of the window. But the importance here is to prioritize this child, rather than casting them aside and concentrating on children who seem to do everything right. Parents have to trust God that things will turn around. The critical thing is factoring in love with everything you do for your children, regardless of how old they are. Having compassion and empathy towards their struggles while also maintaining a constant love for them is crucial to come out on the other side of things more mature, secure and confident.

Teens also suffer, along with common confusion, from low self-esteem and peer pressure. Every teenager is susceptible to self-esteem issues. At this point, your teen's primary concerns are others' opinion, which can take a massive blow to their self-esteem. Teenagerhood introduces a lot of vulnerability that can lead to mental health issues manifesting now or later on in their lives. This is the best time for positive reinforcement because your teen is concerned with the perception that others have on them. This is when parents should be rejoicing in the positive developments that occur in their teen's life.

As parents and adults are concerned, it is our responsibility to encourage teenagers to promote positive self-esteem. It's an evolving process, and there are no shortcuts. It is essential to remind teens on an ongoing basis that they are amazing teenagers and that we are proud of them. Reminding them of their worth and value every day can boost their perceptions of themselves. But it is so much more than just telling them. Showcasing their worth to the entire family dynamic and why they are an essential puzzle piece gives them a better understanding of why they are so loved and cherished as people.

Adopt these tactics every day to increase the self-esteem and confidence of your teenagers:

1. Set your teenager a good example.

No matter how remote the teen can appear, the habits are very closely modelled. If they see that you have a problem with self-esteem, they can imitate that. Set a precedent of a positive attitude for yourself and others. Being a model of expected behaviour is a requirement from the moment your children are born. If you expect them to be polite, you have to be polite as well. This also carries into increasingly challenging and complex subjects like self-esteem as they age. But it is entirely necessary to be able to show your teens an excellent example to follow.

2. When seeking the ability to talk with your kids, lessen the time with teens.

Being able to differentiate when your teens want to speak to you or simply require your presence is an excellent skill to learn. It's up to you to understand your child's nuances to support them in the best way you possibly can. But if your teen changes their minds, they may not want to talk to you, make sure they know you're available. Sometimes, simply feeling that you're there for them makes a difference.

* Part of relating to a teenager is deliberately listening. Teens dealing with self-esteem sometimes believe that no one listens to them or cares about what they have to say. Show them you're listening by letting them finish and then answering questions about what they said. You might be inclined to give them

advice as soon as you understand the issue given that you are an adult with more experience but resist this because the more important thing is to lend an ear to your child and allow them to express themselves to their full extent to get things off of their chest rather than bottling it up, which can do more harm than good.

3. Help set expectations for your child and cheer when they achieve them.

Start with small goals that they can achieve in a short period. Celebrate as they reach the target for them. Keep inspiring them if their target takes longer to complete, and their confidence will grow. A goal-setting mindset helps keep you focused on a bigger picture without getting too overwhelmed. Especially as a teen, ambitions can seem like a massive feat to try and tackle. This method is excellent to teach your teens how to manage their aspirations.

* Let your teen know that adjusting her aim along the way is all right. This is the way of life and an important ability that teens need to learn. When conditions change, we will need to re-adjust our plans. If your teen knows this, it will help build their faith. This is especially crucial because your teens will go through numerous phases and trends as they age into young adulthood. As they are trying to figure out their place in the world, what they may have enjoyed last week may not be relevant this week.

* Teach them that it is just as crucial to take definitive action to achieve their aim as to achieve the goal. Working hard is

essential, and sometimes it isn't emphasized enough. To achieve the goals that they have set, your teens have to accept that it will take effort and discipline to make a real impact. Warning them well-ahead of time and teaching them will set them up for a life that isn't full of disappointments and reality checks.

* Failure at some point is inevitable, so be prepared to address these concerns if the time comes. Patience is crucial here because your teen may be experiencing even more self-doubt, disappointment, and sadness than usual. They may also be secretive of it. This is why it's crucial to have open communication lines that uplift, rather than condemn.

4. Let a teen son know that he makes you to be proud of him.

Tell them just how good they were when they scored an A. It's just as important that your teenager knows that if they get a C, you're still proud of that score. Encourage them to do their best and be proud of them as they do. Avoid tying their worth and value to frivolous things like grades or their appearance. This is a sure way to develop deeply rooted insecurities and follow them for the rest of their lives. Rather than doing so, focus on their qualities and abilities to constantly improve and evolve as a human being. This can be a challenge when as a society we are hyper-focused on determining a person's value through numbers or standards of beauty, but it does not mean that you cannot implement them in your household.

5. Encourage your kid to indulge in new experience they enjoy.

Being outgoing and open to new experiences is a great way to expand your son's horizons even further and expose them to new social, educational, and spiritual situations where they can learn and grow.

That could be any operation, gatherings, club, or organization. Getting them engaged in things would help them see they are more normal than they think they are!

Promote their individuality and interests by allowing them to choose the method. Give them the flexibility to express themselves by being involved in their desires and passions.

Self-expression is vital for teens because it serves as a healthy outlet when times get incredibly stressful or challenging. Encouraging your kid to pursue their interests prioritizes self-care in their own lives shows them that it's okay to take time for themselves and what they care about.

6. Encourage your child to live a healthier lifestyle.

Health is wealth, and encouraging this mindset is crucial for your teen to appreciate and care for their bodies to the best of their abilities.

If young adults are couch potatoes or have unhealthy food habits, problems may also present themselves. When a teen eats a healthy diet and needs a daily amount of exercise, it's easier for them to feel better about themselves. Childhood body dysmorphia is a genuine problem that can worsen during the teenage years. Binge eating, yo-yo dieting, anorexia, obesity and bulimia are every day during teenagerhood and can vary in degree from teenager to teenager. When adults don't prioritize health and demonstrate how important it is to care for your bodies, this reflects poorly on their children. It gives them unhealthy coping mechanisms and poor relationships rooted in abusing food. Meals become a time for managing their feelings, rather than dealing with their issues head-on and discussing the problems they face with a trusted adult. This can all be extremely dangerous for their health. It will take years of recovery to have a better relationship with their bodies if not dealt with accordingly right from the start. Meaning, it is critical that parents exemplify a healthy relationship with food. If parents face hardship with their bodies and food, it is essential to seek the proper help to demonstrate that it is acceptable to get help and guidance.

Arrange for a full check-up for your teen from the hospital. Your primary health care provider should rule out all physical causes for your teen's low self-esteem. They can also recommend more interventions or treatments that could improve the situation.

Set a routine for physical exercise in any form, whether its dance or a sport. Any movement at all is good and will help your teen live and lead a healthier and happier lifestyle.

Self-confidence can be low for teenagers. All the time you expend building, your teen's confidence can be torn down in one crappy afternoon. A small comment or bullying at school can exceptionally be a significant blow on a teen's self-esteem. Either can have varying degrees of severity on your child's perception of themselves. Something as severe as bullying is severe and needs to be dealt with. But the same effect can occur over a nonchalant comment that someone makes about your teen's appearances. Regardless of *how* it may have happened, it is essential to teach your teens healthy ways to cope with these comments. Leaving these unvisited can fester into more significant problems that will manifest later on in life. Having an open conversation with an adult they trust can exponentially improve how your child feels and how they internalize these comments.

There will be bad and great days for teens, just like everyone else. Never excuse or give up on them yourself. Try these strategies, and soon enough, you'll know you're on the right track. Your youth will go through mood swings, but they will emerge as a safe and stable adult with time and focus.

Talk about subjects with adolescents and teach them that learning to deal with rejection, critique, and challenges is a necessary life experience. Chat to your teen about how important it is to know that they are already a great person, worthy of love and attention, no matter what life might throw their way. As a parent, you are your child's cheerleader. Showing them that they are loved unconditionally, regardless of their looks or grades, is crucial to them tying their self-worth to the internal qualities they have.

One thing that is obvious about teenagers is that if they are happy and confident, they do better in all facets of their lives. Having a happy teen on your hands will reflect all other aspects of life, like school and social life. Your teen will have concrete building blocks that lead to a successful future. Adolescent self-esteem or lack of it will have a profoundly detrimental influence on the youth, so it's imperative to help your teen reflect on self-esteem and try to make it low on your teenage problem list!

Training and guiding your child is not forever, and you will notice your influence growing less and less as they tend to age. Since this is a time when they will learn the most in their lives, take advantage of this time to teach your kids to love and spread kindness wherever they go. Creating a solid foundation is rooted in encouraging them to live a healthy lifestyle. This will teach them to value their life, and the time they spend on Earth by doing meaningful things, pleasing their maker and leaving a positive impact upon others no matter where they go.

Control challenges, rudeness, and ignorance

Given that it is normal to feign confusion and refuse to engage in polite conversation during the teen years, how can parents connect successfully with teens to be understood?

This issue is where some of the most volatile arguments and rows can occur between parents and their children. Your teens will employ every trick in the book to get out of consequences and break the rules. Parents have seen it all, from lying to straight-up pretending to have not heard you. The excuses are relentless and can seriously weigh a parent down.

This is where parents need to develop healthy and helpful methods to deal with teens who resist authority. Instead of constantly arguing, try some of these different methods when it comes to dealing with your teens. The goal and most ideal outcome is to be as calm and collected as possible. Acting out of anger will only exacerbate the situation, and you will end up with a more difficult time on your hands.

Here's one way to deal with your teenager's lack of listening abilities: expect to hear you as they do. If you know that your teen has no hearing disorder and does not actually have earphones on and you speak simply in a vocabulary he also uses, assume that he can hear you. Look at him and clearly and calmly state your rules and expectations: "To get a ride in the morning, you must be back home by 9 pm tonight. I know the driving privilege is what you want, so make sure you make it home by 9." Here, the parent has carefully and outlined the terms. Nothing is confusing about this, which is an important detail when your teen tries to ignore the terms you have set, and you are in the midst of an argument. You never want to second guess the rules you have set yourself.

When he insists he didn't hear you when he wanders in at five past ten, instead of moaning about his hearing ability, you can say: "You know the rules. You didn't make it home by 9, but you didn't have a ride in the morning. You'll try tomorrow evening again. You've got the car in by nine the following day." Don't get dragged into a fight with him overpower. Turn around, and if he tries to pull you closer, leave the room.

See how that way works? Only as you sidestep the power struggle over touch forms, you can focus on the problem at hand and do what is right. Do what you can to be clear and direct even when referring to the back of your teenager's head when he stares at a cell phone page. Then, make him accountable for his choices. It's a conversation about a detour, and it won't get you where you need to go. Don't debate whether or not he heard you. Accountability is crucial here. Your teen might try to weasel out of a situation by making excuses and trying to transfer the blame onto something or someone else for fear of punishment. Your way around this is to always be clear in your standards and hold them to it, especially when they go against your explicit instructions.

If your teenager is routinely held responsible, it turns into your teen saying, "But I didn't hear you!" Next time, you could have a little discussion about paying attention and how he could listen differently. Know, you're going to understand everything if you keep your cool and stay focused.

Sometimes your teens have to be reminded that you are the adult, and that respect is a two-way street. In this instance, keeping your cool and not raising your voice is an example of that. As frustrated and stressed out as you may feel, avoid succumbing to these intense emotions because they often lead to even more rebellious and even explosive behaviour from your teens.

To make sure that the message comes out loud and simple, note these tips:

1. Keep your reward before your eyes

What's your goal? What's the only piece of information you want to get from your teenager? State your facts plainly and don't encourage your adolescent to drag you off track.

2. Don't Take it Personally

When your teenager ignores you, yells at you, or pretends not to hear you remember that he is attempting to be more powerful in this situation. Remind yourself that a power struggle or screaming war will only make things worse. Keep calm, even though you are annoyed, and tell the truth. If he intends to pull you near, turn around and leave. You don't have to attend whatever fight you're invited to. Keeping your cool shows your teen that being loud doesn't automatically exempt them from consequences. So, if you need to do so, take a moment to breathe and calm down instead of acting rashly and blindly from your emotions. Ultimately, it will only harm things even more by doing so.

3. Don't be scared of the rules

When your teen lobs a zinger at you to start an argument, hold the conversation focused on your interests, not on your teen's thoughts about justice. When you argue with your teen on the rules, the irony is that it allows him to feel that the rules are changeable. Instead, stick to the truth: "I know that you disagree with the rules, and you would prefer not to listen to me. The irony is that the rules don't have to be liked; you only have to find a way to enforce them.

Know, remain cool, focus on the topic at hand, and encourage your teenager to knock you off the subject. Believe me. The teen knows that scratching his eyes, murmuring under his breath, and having a pessimistic mood makes you irritated. He's doing so on purpose. The more you demand the show of "active listening" (in other words, paying attention respectfully and acknowledging your demand), the more he will fight to ignore you. You're not going there. "Repeat this mantra: " Authority struggles are never a fruitful use of my time.

Regardless of age, your kids need to be met with resistance because it teaches them that ultimately there are consequences to all of our actions. If they are a toddler or a teen, parents need to adapt to this and apply the necessary measures to respect and obey the rules that exist within the household. Obedience can be difficult for teens and parents tend to cast these responsibilities to the father figure within the household. While there is nothing wrong with this inherently, this can affect how your teens perceive their fathers if discipline is always associated with him.

The best advice to curb this is by dividing up the responsibilities among both parents. This instils the idea that discipline is not associated with a single figure but is a universal expectation. While traditional roles would associate mothers with being nurturers and fathers as disciplinary figures, this can create a fissure between parents that carries over to children.

Regardless of how you choose to instil a sense of discipline and responsibility in your house, be sure to be mindful of how your teens receive the expectations. The best way parents have found to work around this is by involving their children insignificant decisions that will affect their lives. For example, while you have the ultimate final say in your teen's curfew, allowing them to negotiate and explain *why* they would like to spend time out later can be a good way for them to be more accepting of what they may see as your sanctions.

Additionally, if you are ever caught up in an argument about curfews, it would be an excellent time to remind them that everyone agreed the time set in the family. Negotiating and compromise are the best ways around difficult decisions. Ultimately, it's about reminding your kids that they have agreed to the terms, and they have to consent to the rules of the family that should be fair to everyone involved.

Control challenges, rudeness, and ignorance

Challenges will occur as you raise your children. This is inevitable. Your boundaries will continuously be tested, and you will face arguments and fights that will frustrate you. Maintaining a positive outlook can be a great challenge, but using positive language is incredibly important for your child's development, especially when dealing with sibling relationships. Parents struggle with this the most because sibling dynamics can be complicated and challenging to navigate through.

For parents, navigating through their children's dynamics is the root of a lot of household problems. Kids can be vicious, and for one set of parents, their son and daughter's relationship was too volatile to the point where they found no moment of peace in their household. Tom and Kelly were Will and Tiffany's parents and were at wits end when solving their kids' problems. They found that their older son Will and the younger daughter Tiffany could not come to terms with each other no matter what they did. They only seemed to be on relatively favourable terms on Christmas Day. The rest of the year was met with arguments, fighting, and tears from Tiffany because they argued about everything and anything. How did Tom and Kelly come to resolve the plight of their children? By following a lot of the tips and steps that are outlined in this chapter. Tom and Kelly had to regain control over their household and set strict rules in their home that had consequences for both of the siblings. They found that as parents, they had perhaps been too lenient with their kids, which led to disrespect behaviour and acting out from both of them. The best means of tackling this was limiting their kids' freedoms to understand that there are consequences to their poor behaviour. Tom and Kelly regained their confidence as parents and were able to set behavioural guidelines for their kids. While Tom and Kelly expected them to be old enough to know the difference between right and wrong, sometimes as parents you might have to go back to basics and essentially treat your teens like children again for them to see how ridiculous and out of line their behaviour is. Don't be afraid to discipline your children, no matter how old they get. Immediately, Tom and Kelly saw a change in their actions as they realized how childish and immature their arguments were affecting everyone in the household. For both parents and children, it was a wakeup call.

The focus is to train your sons during the most formative years of their lives to obey instruction and thus lay a solid foundation for them to thrive and evolve into human beings that have all of the good qualities. Letting a young and impressionable child have his way is a recipe for disaster as it leads to disobedience and developing the wrong building on the faulty foundation. Tom and Kelly found themselves in the face of education as well. Part of the root reasoning for the dysfunctionality within their family was that they could not decide on a parenting style that suited each parent. They finally arrived (after much trial and error) to the counsel they had received where fathers give explicit instruction or guidelines, and mothers teach by breaking fathers instructions into bite-size that is easy for the children to obey. Will and Tiffany's parents took the time to understand their relationship dynamics to help their household members. They were able to work together to break it down so the kids could obey. Fostering respect in a household is paramount, and doing so might not be an easy task when you have rebellious teenagers on your hands. Parents must teach their children to honour each other from a young age, and children must understand the social norm of speaking respectfully to parents throughout their lives.

Please Leave a 1-click Review!

I would be incredibly thankful if you could take just 60 seconds to write a brief review on the platform of purchase, even if it's just a few sentences!

Conclusion

Raising Sons and daughters can be equally as challenging and fighting the gender roles assigned to them can be extremely difficult as your child enters the education system and faces various influences in their lives that will constantly reiterate these labels. However, establishing that your sons can flourish and respect their way of life is the first step to breaking down some of the societal expectations that are simply unrealistic and illogical. The fact that cooking has historically been deemed a "woman's job" is unrealistic in the twenty-first century and beyond. To raise self-sufficient and responsible sons, rid yourself of the inherent biases you may have and focus on wholeheartedly bringing up your teen sons to succeed in their lives in whatever way they choose to do so. Instead of encouraging them to follow the status quo, provide them with the tools they need to nurture their likes and dislikes.

Teen boys are faced with their own set of identity-related issues as they grapple with the framework of masculinity that is imposed on them. Some boys choose to act within this framework, while others choose not.

Parents are to pray for them, encourage and guide them with their decisions and be their cheerleader. Help them nurture their instincts, follow the leading of their conscience, which gets more sensitive as they read and follow the scriptures.

Young people have so much untapped potential that society will end up stifling because of the strict norms that are continuously enforced through its institutions like schools and the workforce. These highly gendered environments emphasize traditional male and female stereotypes which greatly limit teens all together. It can have a severe effect on a person's well-being and hinder confidence. However, this can all be controlled and completely disregarded in the household, where parents can control the message they want to send out to their children. Rather than focusing on these traditional stereotypes, choosing to instead foster true-love and confidence in your abilities is an excellent way to teach your children that it is perfectly acceptable to be themselves, no matter what society may tell them.

Toxic masculinity can subconsciously worm its way into your teen's consciousness through social media or even their peers and the interactions that they have. Establishing early on that this is a harmful way of thinking can save your teenage son a lot of grief and hardship as they grapple with their identity in the process of maturing and ageing. Establish that they are not defined by society's harmful standards of masculinity and encourage them to develop their own identity that they are comfortable with and proud of from their maker's perspective, which is known more when they read the scriptures...

The challenge comes in at the vital part of successfully raising sons (and children in general), which is to strike a balance between allowing them to express themselves freely and disciplining them should they cross the line. It is a complicated task that many parents find daunting and at times, impossible to do. But now, armed with the tips and techniques of these books, you will be able to find that balance in your household to raise sons that follow the appropriate conventions of life while also flourishing in their own space.

While this book discusses disciplining teens and how parents can be extremely frustrated or angered by behaviours, it is also crucial to note how parenting itself is an incredible privilege and a joy as you watch your teens grow and develop. Parents can see the pieces of knowledge that they imparted on their kids from a young age come out when they are older, and the pride associated with your child growing up to be good people is indescribable. Disciplining your children can seem like a dreaded thing, but it is merely one of the many facets that are part of being a parent. There are always going to be upsides and downsides to everything.

Parents need to realize that this is a normal process boys go through, through their adulthood progression. A fascinating, but the explosive combination is produced by the mix of testosterone running through their bloodstream and a natural desire to differentiate from their parents.

You look at your son, and you ask him to do a job. In a rage, he cries out. His poor language abilities stop him from being able to communicate his thoughts or describe them. You take this reaction as a personal assault and some kind of flaw in your son. Take a look back and slowly breathe. This condition has arisen since there were teenage boys on the first day.

The teenage boy is seen stereotypically as a wild, rebellious adolescent who is always in conflict with his parents. Although adolescent boys have their emotional ups and downs, they have a practical and compassionate side.

Developing freedom is the main force for adolescents. Informs that would frustrate kin, this is embodied. A boy who usually conforms to his parents' wishes will unexpectedly show himself and share his views. They strongly protest against the control of their parents and establish a moral code of their own.

Parents need to step back to realize that they need to build and create their own lives for teens (boys and girls). Do you listen to your kids as their feelings and ideas are expressed? Do you make it easy for them to have differing views and thoughts than yours? As you will for every other human, you ought to respect their opinions and viewpoints. For harmful or destructive wishes/thoughts, sound parental decision and interference are, of course, to be required.

Other Books You'll Love!

1. Raising Boys in Today's Digital World: Proven Positive Parenting Tips for Raising Respectful, Successful and Confident Boys
2. Raising Girls in Today's Digital World: Proven Positive Parenting Tips for Raising Respectful, Successful and Confident Girls
3. Raising Kids in Today's Digital World: Proven Positive Parenting Tips for Raising Respectful, Successful and Confident Kids
4. The Child Development and Positive Parenting Master Class 2-in-1 Bundle: Proven Methods for Raising Well-Behaved and Intelligent Children, with Accelerated Learning Methods
5. Parenting Teens in Today's Challenging World 2-in-1 Bundle: Proven Methods for Improving Teenagers Behaviour with Positive Parenting and Family Communication
6. Life Strategies for Teenagers: Positive Parenting, Tips and Understanding Teens for Better Communication

and a Happy Family
7. Parenting Teen Girls in Today's Challenging World: Proven Methods for Improving Teenagers Behaviour with Whole Brain Training
8. Parenting Teen Boys in Today's Challenging World: Proven Methods for Improving Teenagers Behaviour with Whole Brain Training
9. 101 Tips For Helping With Your Child's Learning: Proven Strategies for Accelerated Learning and Raising Smart Children Using Positive Parenting Skills
10. 101 Tips for Child Development: Proven Methods for Raising Children and Improving Kids Behavior with Whole Brain Training
11. Financial Tips to Help Kids: Proven Methods for Teaching Kids Money Management and Financial Responsibility
12. Healthy Habits for Kids: Positive Parenting Tips for Fun Kids Exercises, Healthy Snacks, and Improved Kids Nutrition
13. Mini Habits for Happy Kids: Proven Parenting Tips for Positive Discipline and Improving Kids' Behavior
14. Good Habits for Healthy Kids 2-in-1 Combo Pack: Proven Positive Parenting Tips for Improving Kids Fitness and Children's Behavior
15. Raising Teenagers to Choose Wisely: Keeping your Teen Secure in a Big World
16. Tips for #CollegeLife: Powerful College Advice for Excelling as a College Freshman
17. The Career Success Formula: Proven Career

Development Advice and Finding Rewarding Employment for Young Adults and College Graduates
18. The Motivated Young Adult's Guide to Career Success and Adulthood: Proven Tips for Becoming a Mature Adult, Starting a Rewarding Career and Finding Life Balance
19. Bedtime Stories for Kids: Short Funny Stories and poems Collection for Children and Toddlers
20. Guide for Boarding School Life
21. The Fear of The Lord: How God's Honour Guarantees Your Peace

22. Spelling for Kids: An Interactive Vocabulary and Spelling Workbook for Kids Ages 5-13

Facebook Community[1]

I will like to invite you to our Facebook community group to visit this link and simply click the join group.

https://www.facebook.com/groups/397683731371863

This is a private group where parents, teachers and carers can learn, share tips, ask questions, discuss and get valuable content about raising and parent modern children. It is a very supportive and encouraging group where valuable content, free resources and exciting discussion about parenting is being shared. You can use this to benefit from social media. You will be learning a lot from school teachers, experts, counsellors, new and experienced parents, and stay updated with our latest releases.

See you there!

---

1. https://www.facebook.com/groups/397683731371863

References

[1] https://cchp.ucsf.edu/sites/g/files/tkssra181/f/SelfEsteem_en0710.pdf

[2] https://www.theseus.fi/bitstream/handle/10024/50239/Anttila_Marianna_Saikkonen_Pinja.pdf

[3] https://ijcat.com/archives/volume5/issue2/ijcatr05021006.pdf

[4] https://www.harvey.k-state.edu/family-and-consumer-sciences/family_and_child_development/documents/CommunicatingwTeenTrust.pdf

[5] https://www.researchgate.net/publication/283721084_Early_Reading_Development

[6] https://www.understood.org/en/friends-feelings/empowering-your-child/building-on-strengths/download-hands-on-activity-to-identify-your-childs-strengths

[7] https://www.wfm.noaa.gov/pdfs/ParentingYourTeen_Handout1.pdf

[8] https://www.helpguide.org/articles/depression/parents-guide-to-teen-depression.htm?pdf=13027

[9] https://www2.ed.gov/parents/academic/help/adolescence/adolescence.pdf

[10] http://centerforchildwelfare.org/kb/prprouthome/Helping%20Your%20Children%20Navigate%20Their%20Teenage%2

[11] https://www.childrensmn.org/images/family_resource_pdf/027121.pdf

[12] https://educationnorthwest.org/sites/default/files/developing-empathy-in-children-and-youth.pdf

[13] http://drkateaubrey.com/wp-content/uploads/2016/02/Parenting-Your-Strong-Willed-Child.pdf

[14] https://www.researchgate.net/publication/263227023_Family_Time_Activities_and_Adolescents'_Emotion

[15] https://parenting-ed.org/wp-content/themes/parenting-ed/files/handouts/communication-parent-to-child.pdf

[16] https://www.wikihow.mom/Trust-Your-Teenager

[17] https://www.statmodel.com/download/Meeus,%20vd%20Schoot,%20Klimstra%20&.pdf

[18] https://www.nap.edu/resource/19401/ProfKnowCompFINAL.pdf

[19] http://www.delmarlearning.com/companions/content/1418019224/AdditionalSupport/box11.1.pdf

[20] http://resources.beyondblue.org.au/prism/file?token=BL/1810_A

[21] https://exeter.anglican.org/wp-content/uploads/2014/11/Listening-to-children-leaflet_NCB.pdf

[22] https://www.researchgate.net/publication/312600262_Creative_Thinking_among_Preschool_Children

[23] https://www.gutenberg.org/files/15114/15114-pdf.pdf

[24] https://discovery.ucl.ac.uk/id/eprint/1522668/1/Thesis%20Moulton%20V%20281016.pdf

[25] https://www.bda.uk.com/foodfacts/healthyeatingchildren.pdf

[26] http://www.tuskmont.org/uploads/1/7/7/2/17728377/follow_the_child_trust_the_child.pdf

[27] https://www.apa.org/pi/families/resources/develop.pdf

[28] https://extension.colostate.edu/docs/pubs/consumer/10249.pdf

[29] https://www.empoweringparents.com/article/risky-teen-behavior-can-you-trust-your-child-again/

[30] http://www.wecf.eu/download/2018/05%20May/WSSPPublicationENPartC-MHMchapter.pdf

Milton Keynes UK
Ingram Content Group UK Ltd.
UKHW020659290124
436892UK00018B/584